The Storybook Cookbook

The
Storybook Cookbook

BY

CAROL MacGREGOR

ILLUSTRATED BY RAY CRUZ

DOUBLEDAY & COMPANY, INC.

GARDEN CITY, NEW YORK

Grateful acknowledgment is made to the following for permission to use copy-righted text and for permission to do new drawings based on the characters from the original illustrations.

Thomas Y. Crowell Company—from *Onion John* by Joseph Krumgold. Illustrated by Symeon Shimin. Copyright © 1959 by Joseph Krumgold.

Doubleday & Company, Inc.—from *Thee, Hannah!* by Marguerite de Angeli. Illustrated by the author. Copyright 1940 by Marguerite de Angeli.

Harper & Row, Publishers, Incorporated—from *Little House in the Big Woods* by Laura Ingalls Wilder. Illustrated by Garth Williams. Copyright 1932 by Laura Ingalls Wilder.

Christopher Lofting—from *The Story of Dr. Dolittle* by Hugh Lofting. Illustrated by the author. Copyright 1948 by Josephine Lofting. Copyright 1920 by Hugh Lofting.

Rand McNally & Company—from *Misty of Chincoteague* by Marguerite Henry. Illustrated by Wesley Dennis. Copyright 1947 by Rand McNally & Company.

Charles Scribner's Sons—from *Peter Pan* by James M. Barrie. Illustrated by Nora Unwin. From *The Wind in the Willows* by Kenneth Grahame. Illustrated by Ernest H. Shepard.

The Viking Press, Inc.—from *Homer Price* by Robert McCloskey. Illustrated by the author. Copyright 1943 by Robert McCloskey. From *Rabbit Hill* by Robert Lawson. Illustrated by the author. Copyright 1944 by Robert Lawson. From *Roller Skates* by Ruth Sawyer. Illustrated by Valenti Angelo. Copyright 1936, 1964 by Ruth Sawyer.

A. Watkins, Inc.—from *The Secret Garden* by Frances Hodgson Burnett. Illustrated by Tasha Tudor. Copyright 1911 by F. H. Burnett; copyright renewal 1918 by Verity Constance Burnett.

To NANA,
who taught me how to cook, and
to POLLY ANNE,
who tested the recipes for
other children

Contents

Introduction

It's fun to cook, and it's amazing to discover how many different kinds of foods there are and, with a little practice, how many exciting dishes you can make. The recipes in this cookbook are for foods that favorite storybook characters have eaten—Heidi's Toasted Cheese Sandwiches, Captain Hook's Poison Cake, Hans Brinker's Waffles, Pinocchio's Poached Eggs, and many more. There are brief descriptions of all the stories, quotes from the books about the foods, and then recipes to follow—for cakes, pies, pretzels, fried chicken, and pot pie.

If you've never cooked before, you'll need some help. But once you've separated an egg, or kneaded bread or beaten whites of eggs, you will be able to do it alone the next time.

Before you start to cook, read any recipe all the way through. And get out all the utensils and ingredients you will need in advance, for once you begin, there may not be time to stop to look for something you want. If there are any recipe terms you don't understand, turn to the glossary at the back of the book, where you'll find a definition of the word or procedure.

It's a good idea, too, to wash the pots and pans as you go along. It's much easier to cook in a kitchen that is neat and clean. A clutter of dirty dishes makes for confusion.

Pinocchio's Pannikin Poached Egg

from THE ADVENTURES OF PINOCCHIO
by Carlo Collodi

Geppetto decided to make a beautiful wooden puppet and travel around the world with it to earn his living. He lovingly carved it from what seemed to be an ordinary piece of wood, but as he shaped the nose, it began to grow—and it grew until it was immense. That wasn't all! When the mouth was complete, Pinocchio began to tease poor Geppetto, and as soon as he'd learned to walk, the puppet ran off into the street. He was at once caught by a policeman, but as the angry Geppetto tried to take him home, Pinocchio convinced the crowds that Geppetto was a tyrant and should be taken to prison. Then the ungrateful and mischievous puppet returned home, tired and hungry, and desperately looked about for something to eat.

13

Just then he thought he saw something in the dust heap—
something round and white that looked like a hen's egg. To
give a spring and seize hold of it was the affair of a moment.
It was indeed an egg.

Pinocchio's joy beats description; it can only be imagined.
Almost believing it must be a dream, he kept turning the egg
over in his hands, feeling it and kissing it. And as he kissed
it he said:

"And now, how shall I cook it? Shall I make an omelet?
No, it would be better to cook it in a saucer! Or would it not
be more savory to fry it in the frying-pan? Or shall I simply
boil it? No, the quickest way of all is to cook it in a pannikin:
I am in such a hurry to eat it!"

Without loss of time he placed a pannikin on a brazier
full of red-hot embers. Into the pannikin instead of oil or
butter he poured a little water; and when the water began to
smoke, tac! he broke the eggshell over it that the contents
might drop in. But instead of the white and the yolk, a little
chicken popped out very gay and polite.

Unlike Pinocchio, you can't expect to find a little chicken in
your egg, but you can do what Pinocchio was planning to
do with his precious egg—poach it. Here's how to prepare
one—and you can use a small pan (pannikin) and stove
(instead of embers).

INGREDIENTS

1 teaspoon vinegar
1 or 2 eggs for each
person
1 or 2 pieces of toast for
each person
Butter
Salt
Pepper

UTENSILS

Frying pan
Measuring spoons
Large spoon
Toaster
Dull knife
Slotted spoon

1. Put about one inch of water in a frying pan, and add
the vinegar. Bring the water to a brisk boil.

14

2. Lower the heat and bring the water to a simmer. Crack the eggs one at a time on the edge of the frying pan and slip them into the water.

3. Spoon a little of the hot water over the top of the eggs and cook them until the whites and yolks of the eggs are firm, but not hard.

4. While the eggs are cooking, make one or two pieces of toast for each egg you are poaching. Butter the toast with the dull knife and place the pieces on plates.

5. With a slotted spoon, lift the eggs out of the water one at a time and put them on the toast. Sprinkle with a little salt and pepper and serve.

Hans's Waffles

from HANS BRINKER or THE SILVER SKATES
by Mary Mapes Dodge

Hans and Gretel Brinker lived in Amsterdam with their invalid
father and their mother, who worked very hard to keep the
family together. It was Christmas, or the Feast of Saint
Nicholas as it was known to them, and the family was too
poor to celebrate the holiday with gifts. But Dame Brinker
wanted the children to have *some* joy on the holiday, and
she knit a pair of socks for Hans to sell in the market.
With the money, he would buy waffles as a special treat.
And some wealthy children had given Hans money for a pair
of ice skates so he could compete in the exciting race for
the Silver Skates. It would not be such a ·sad Christmas
after all!

*That will give us three quarter-guilders if you make good
trade; and as it's right hungry weather, you may buy four
waffles. We'll keep the Feast of Saint Nicholas after all."*

Gretel clapped her hands. "That will be fine! Annie Bouman told me what grand times they will have in the big houses tonight. But we will be merry, too. Hans will have beautiful new skates—and then there'll be the waffles! Oh-h! Don't break them, brother Hans. Wrap them well, and button them under your jacket very carefully."

"Certainly," replied Hans, quite gruff with pleasure and importance.

Waffles are a traditional food in Holland. They are warm and toasty in cold weather such as Hans and Gretel knew, but they are also good in summer with cold honey or jam served on top. Like Hans, you do have to be careful not to break them.

INGREDIENTS

3 eggs
1¼ cups milk
¼ cup butter
2 cups sifted flour
2 teaspoons baking powder
½ teaspoon salt
2 teaspoons sugar

UTENSILS

Waffle iron
Large bowl
Measuring cup
Beater
Small saucepan
Large spoon
Flour sifter
Measuring spoons
Fork

1. Start heating a waffle iron to medium heat (on many irons, you can set the temperature with a button).

2. Crack the eggs on the side of a large bowl and drop them into the bowl. Add the milk and mix the eggs and milk together with a beater.

3. Put the butter in a small saucepan and melt it over low heat. Be careful not to burn it. With a large spoon, slowly stir the butter into the egg mixture.

4. Presift the flour. Then sift the measured flour with the baking powder, salt, and sugar. Stir thoroughly into the egg mixture.

5. Melt a little butter on the waffle iron. Fill the lower section of the waffle iron about half full with the batter. Bring the cover down and cook until lightly browned—about 5 minutes. Loosen the edges of the waffle with a fork and carefully remove it. Serve with syrup, honey, or jam. Makes about 6 waffles.

Dorothy's Scrambled Eggs

from THE WIZARD OF OZ by L. Frank Baum

Dorothy found herself in quite a predicament when her house was swept away by a cyclone and set down in the strange land of the Munchkins. She had to find a way back to her aunt and uncle in Kansas, and with her little dog, Toto, she set out for the Emerald City to find the wonderful Wizard. The Wizard, she was told, would help her get home, but the yellow brick road was full of dangers. Along the way she made three friends who also needed the Wizard's help: the Scarecrow, who wanted a brain; the Tin Woodman, who had lost his heart; and the Lion, who lacked courage. After many adventures they arrived exhausted at the Land of Oz and stopped at the nearest farmhouse before going to see the Wizard.

The woman now called to them that supper was ready, so they gathered around the table and Dorothy ate some de-

licious porridge and a dish of scrambled eggs and a plate of nice white bread, and enjoyed her meal. The Lion ate some of the porridge, but did not care for it, saying it was made from oats and oats were food for horses, not for lions. The Scarecrow and the Tin Woodman ate nothing at all. Toto ate a little of everything, and was glad to get a good supper again.

Well, anything can happen in Oz. We would probably call their meal a breakfast rather than a "supper." Try making the scrambled eggs.

INGREDIENTS

6 large eggs
2 tablespoons heavy or
   light cream (or milk)
¼ teaspoon salt
Shake of pepper
2 tablespoons butter

UTENSILS

Small bowl
Fork
Measuring spoons
Frying pan
Large spoon

1. Break the eggs into a small bowl and beat with a fork until they are well mixed.

2. Stir in the cream, salt, and pepper.

3. Put a frying pan on the stove and turn the heat on low. Melt the butter in the pan, but do not let it turn brown.

4. Pour the eggs into the pan. Cook, stirring with a large spoon, until the eggs are set. Spoon onto plates. Makes 3 or 4 servings.

Uncle Ulysses' Doughnuts

from HOMER PRICE by Robert McCloskey

It all started because Uncle Ulysses loved laborsaving devices, particularly those which made his lunchroom in Centerburg run more smoothly. He'd invested in an automatic doughnut-making machine, and when Homer visited him one evening, his uncle left him to put the last two pieces of the machine together and then mix up a batch. Having assembled the machine, Homer was about to mix the batter when a wealthy lady pulled up in a large black car. Seeing the situation, she volunteered:

*N*ow, *young man, you simply must allow me to help. You know, I haven't made doughnuts for years, but I know the best recipe for doughnuts. It's marvelous, and we really must use it.*"

"*But, Ma'm . . ." said Homer.*

"*Now just* wait *till you taste these doughnuts," said the lady. "Do you have an apron?" she asked, as she took off her fur coat and her rings and her jewelry and rolled up her sleeves. "Charles," she said to the chauffeur, "hand me that baking powder, that's right, and, young man, we'll need some nutmeg."*

So Homer and the chauffeur stood by and handed things and cracked the eggs while the lady mixed and stirred. Mr. Gabby sat on his stool, sipped his coffee, and looked on with great interest.

"There!" said the lady when all of the ingredients were mixed. "Just wait *till you taste these doughnuts!"*

"It looks like an awful lot of batter," said Homer as he stood on the edge of the chair and poured it into the doughnut machine with the help of the chauffeur. "It's about ten *times as much as Uncle Ulysses ever makes."*

"But wait till you taste them!" said the lady with an eager look and a smile.

It certainly was a lot of batter—they lost count of the doughnuts at twelve hundred and two! This recipe will make about a dozen, but you may find them so good that you'll decide to make ten times as many, too.

INGREDIENTS	UTENSILS
2 cups sifted flour	Measuring cup
2½ teaspoons baking powder	Measuring spoons
	Flour sifter
¼ teaspoon cinnamon	2 large bowls
¼ teaspoon nutmeg	Beater
½ teaspoon salt	Large spoon
1 egg	Breadboard
½ cup sugar	Rolling pin
1½ tablespoons shortening, room temperature	Dull knife
	Doughnut cutter
½ cup milk	Large, deep frying pan
Can of shortening for frying	Fork
	Paper towels
	Large plate

24

1. Presift the flour. Sift the measured flour with the baking powder, cinnamon, nutmeg, and salt into a large bowl.

2. In another large bowl, beat the egg until light and lemon colored. Beat in the sugar gradually and then add the shortening.

3. Gradually add the flour mixture and the milk alternately, a little at a time, to the egg mixture. Stir thoroughly with a large spoon after you add each small amount. Chill the dough for half an hour in the refrigerator.

4. Sprinkle a little flour on a breadboard so the dough won't stick on it. Place the dough on the board. With a floured rolling pin, roll out the dough into a large circle about $1/4$-inch thick. If the dough sticks to the rolling pin or breadboard, scrape it off carefully with a dull knife and sprinkle more flour on the pin and board. With a doughnut cutter, cut out as many doughnuts as you can—about 12.

5. Put a large, deep frying pan on the stove and turn the heat quite high. Put enough shortening in the pan so that you have about $2\frac{1}{2}$ inches of melted fat. Heat the fat until it begins to pop and snap. Be very careful with it.

6. Drop the doughnuts and the "holes" into the fat very carefully. Fry 3 or 4 at a time for a few minutes on each side until they are golden brown, turning them carefully with a fork.

7. Put some paper towels on a large plate. When the doughnuts finish frying, drain them quickly on the paper. Makes about 12 doughnuts.

Heidi's
Toasted Cheese Sandwiches

from HEIDI by Johanna Spyri

The people of Dörfli were shocked that Heidi was going to live with her grandfather high up the Alp mountains. With his thick gray eyebrows, heavy beard, and his solitary ways, the old man frightened the villagers, and they thought his cottage was no place for a child. But Heidi was delighted by Grandfather's crude but cozy home. First they made a comfortable bed of hay for her by the window in the cottage hayloft where she could look out over the whole valley. Then Grandfather said he thought it was time for supper.

In her eagerness over the bed, Heidi has forgotten everything else; but now that eating was suggested to her, a great feeling of hunger rose within her, for she had taken nothing all day, except a piece of bread and a cup of weak coffee early in the morning, and afterward she had made the long journey.

"Yes, I think so, too."

"Well, let us go down, since we are agreed," said the old man and followed close upon the child's steps. He went to the fireplace, pushed the large kettle aside and drew forward the little one that hung on the chain, sat down on the three-legged wooden stool with the round seat and kindled a bright fire. Almost immediately the kettle began to boil, and the old man held over the fire a large piece of cheese on the end of a long iron fork. He moved it this way and that, until it was golden yellow on all sides. Heidi looked on with eager attention. Suddenly a new idea came to her mind; she jumped up and ran to the cupboard, and kept going back and forth. When the grandfather brought the toasted cheese to the table, it was already nicely laid with the round loaf of bread, two plates, and two knives, for Heidi had noticed everything in the cupboard, and knew that all would be needed for the meal.

"Now, this is nice that you can think of things yourself," said the old man, and put the cheese upon the bread.

Cooking has advanced quite a bit since Heidi's day. But the idea of toasted cheese sandwiches already was well established then. You can make, and even improve upon, this tasty snack from the mountains of Switzerland. You don't need an open fire. The recipe will show you how to prepare a delightful variation of this Alpine treat right in your kitchen.

INGREDIENTS

2 eggs
¾ cup milk
½ teaspoon salt
4 slices Swiss cheese or
   8 slices American cheese
8 slices white bread
4 tablespoons butter
Currant jelly (optional)

UTENSILS

Piepan
Fork
Measuring cup
Measuring spoons
Frying pan
Metal spatula

1. Crack the eggs on the edge of a piepan and drop them into the pan. Beat the eggs slightly with a fork. Stir in the milk and the salt.

2. Make the cheese sandwiches by putting one slice of Swiss cheese folded in half or two slices of American cheese between two slices of bread. (American cheese has a stronger flavor.)

3. Put a frying pan on the stove and turn the heat to medium. Melt 2 tablespoons of the butter in the pan, but do not let it burn.

4. Dip the sandwiches on both sides in the egg-and-milk mixture. Let them soak a minute. When the butter is hot, brown 2 of the sandwiches on both sides, turning them with a spatula. Add the rest of the butter to the frying pan and brown the last 2 sandwiches. A teaspoon of currant jelly on top of each sandwich makes them even tastier. Makes 4 sandwiches.

The
Swiss Family Robinson's
Lobster Bisque

from SWISS FAMILY ROBINSON
by Johann David Wyss

Their ship wrecked in a raging storm, the Swiss Family Robinson found themselves marooned on a desert island. To survive, they had to be resourceful, and they learned to make their own bread, boats, and pottery. They built a tree house to protect themselves from wild animals at night and tamed an ostrich to ride on around the island. When one of the boys accidentally stepped on a lobster, they put *it* to good use, too.

I was startled by hearing Jack shouting for help, as though in great danger. He was at some distance, and I hurried toward him with a hatchet in my hand. The little fellow stood screaming in a deep pool, and as I approached, I saw that a huge lobster had caught his leg in its powerful claw. Poor Jack was in a terrible fright; kick as he would, his enemy still clung on. I waded into the water, and seizing the lobster firmly by the back, managed to make it loosen its hold, and we brought it safe to land. Jack, having speedily recovered his spirits, and anxious to take such a prize to his mother, caught the lobster in both hands, but instantly received such a severe blow from its tail that he flung it down, and passionately hit the creature with a large stone. This display of temper vexed me. "You are acting in a very childish way, my son," said I; "never strike an enemy in a revengeful spirit." Once more lifting the lobster, Jack ran triumphantly toward the tent.

"Mother, mother! a lobster, Ernest! look here, Franz! mind he'll bite you! Where's Fritz?" All came crowding round Jack and his prize, wondering at its unusual size, and Ernest wanted his mother to make lobster soup directly, by adding it to what she was now boiling.

You don't need to catch your own lobster, but you can make this delicious seaside soup.

INGREDIENTS
1 ½ tablespoons butter
2 tablespoons flour
½ teaspoon salt
A dash of pepper
1 ½ cups light cream
½ cup milk
10 oz. of canned lobster
  meat
Red coloring (optional)

UTENSILS
Medium-sized saucepan
Measuring spoons
Large spoon
Measuring cup
Can opener
Medium-sized bowl
Sieve

1. Put a medium-sized saucepan on the stove and turn the heat on low. Melt the butter in the pan, but do not let it burn.

2. Add the flour, salt, and pepper to the butter. Stir over low heat until you have a paste.

3. Gradually add the cream and milk, stirring constantly until the mixture thickens. You may have to turn up the heat a little to thicken the sauce.

4. Open the can of lobster meat and drain off all the liquid. Break the lobster into pieces, and be sure there are no little scales in it. Add it to the cream sauce and cook for 10 minutes.

5. Place a sieve over a medium-sized bowl and pour the lobster bisque into the sieve. With a spoon, press as much of the sauce and lobster meat as you can through the sieve. Discard the remaining lobster meat or feed it to your cat.

6. If you want to, add 2 drops of red coloring to give the soup a nice pink color.

7. Pour the bisque back into the saucepan and reheat it, as it will have cooled off. Serve it hot. Makes 4 servings.

Sailor's Chipped Beef

from TREASURE ISLAND
by Robert Louis Stevenson

One of the most exciting treasure hunts of all time begins
when young Jim Hawkins signs up as a cabin boy on the
Hispaniola. With a few trusted friends, Jim set sail for
Treasure Island to find the buried gold of the famous buc-
caneer Captain Flint. But Long John Silver, the one-legged
sea cook, led the crew to mutiny, and the trip nearly ended in
disaster. Just before the final lap of the hunt, the reckless
pirate crew prepare a typical seaman's breakfast.

*A man hailed us from the fire that breakfast was ready,
and we were soon seated here and there about the sand over
biscuit and fried junk. They had lit a fire fit to roast an ox;
and it was now grown so hot that they could only approach it
from the windward, and even there not without precaution. In*

the same wasteful spirit, they had cooked, I suppose, three times more than we could eat; and one of them, with an empty laugh, threw what was left into the fire, which blazed and roared again over this unusual fuel. I never in my life saw men so careless of the morrow; hand to mouth is the only word that can describe their way of doing.

Fried junk is a dried salted beef that sailors take on voyages with them because it will not spoil easily. The closest food to it that you can fix is chipped beef, which you can cream and serve on toast for lunch or dinner.

Ingredients	Utensils
1 cup milk	Measuring cup
1 cup heavy or light cream	Medium-sized saucepan
	Large frying pan
3 tablespoons butter	Measuring spoons
3 tablespoons flour	Large Spoon
½ teaspoon salt	Toaster
1 cup shredded chipped beef	
4 slices white bread	

1. Put the milk and cream in a medium-sized saucepan. Put the saucepan on the stove and turn the heat on medium. Bring the liquid to a boil and then turn off the heat.

2. Put a large frying pan on the stove and turn the heat on low. Melt the butter in the pan, but do not let it brown.

3. Add the flour to the butter and stir over low heat until the mixture forms a paste. Gradually add the hot milk and cream, stirring constantly until the mixture thickens.

4. Add the salt and the chipped beef and heat until the mixture is hot.

5. Toast the bread and put one slice on each plate. Spoon the chipped beef onto the toast and serve. Makes 4 servings.

Chincoteague Pot Pie

from MISTY OF CHINCOTEAGUE
by Marguerite Henry

Pony Penning Day was a favorite holiday on Chincoteague Island, and Paul and Maureen could hardly wait for it to come. Every year the men of Chincoteague rounded up a herd of wild ponies from a nearby island, and then tried roping and riding the wilder ones—all for the fun of it. Finally, some of the ponies were sold at auction. The men had tried to capture the beautiful mare Phantom for two years without success, and Paul and Maureen had their hearts set on capturing *and* buying her. It's exciting reading to find out what happens to Phantom and her colt, Misty, but one thing is sure —the Pony Penning Day dinner was delicious.

The ladies of the auxiliary hovered over them anxiously, heaping their plates with oysters and clam fritters, and great helpings of Chincoteague pot pie.

The ladies of the auxiliary of Chincoteague sent this authentic recipe for their pot pie, which they actually cook on Pony Penning Day. This is not really pie as you know it, but chicken stew with dumplings. It is good eaten outdoors in the summer or indoors in the winter, but whenever you serve it, you can tell the story of this holiday.

Ingredients	Utensils
Parsley ⎫	3-quart kettle
1 carrot ⎬ optional	String
Celery leaves ⎭	Medium-sized bowl
1 2-lb. chicken, cut into	Measuring cup
pieces	Measuring spoons
Salt	Flour sifter
Pepper	Large spoon
2 cups sifted flour	Dull knife
2 teaspoons baking powder	Breadboard
¼ teaspoon salt	Rolling pin
3 tablespoons shortening	Large fork
½ cup water	Serving plate
	Spatula

1. Fill a large kettle about ¾ full with warm water and put it on the stove. Turn the heat to high.

2. *Tie together a sprig of parsley, a slice of carrot, and a few celery leaves with string and add to the water. Cover the pot and bring the water to a boil.

3. While waiting for the water to boil, sprinkle the chicken pieces on both sides with salt and pepper.

4. When the water is boiling, lift the cover carefully, turning the lid away from you so that the steam will not hit your face. Put the cover down on the edge of the stove. Drop the chicken pieces in very carefully so as not to splash the water. Put the cover back on, turn the heat down to medium, and cook the chicken for 30 minutes.

* Not given in original recipe, but makes chicken tastier.

5. While the chicken is cooking, make the dumplings. Presift the flour and then sift the measured flour with the baking powder and ¼ teaspoon of salt into a medium-sized bowl. Add the shortening. Rub the flour and the shortening lightly through your fingers until they are well-mixed—the crumbs should be the size of small peas.

6. Add the water gradually, cutting it into the flour with a dull knife until the dough sticks together to form a ball.

7. Put the dough on a well-floured breadboard. With a floured rolling pin, roll out the dough into a large circle about ¼-inch thick. If the dough sticks to the rolling pin or breadboard, scrape it off carefully with a dull knife and sprinkle more flour on the pin and board. Cut the dough into 3-inch squares with a dull knife.

8. When the chicken has cooked for 30 minutes, remove the parsley and carrot bundle. Using a spatula, drop the dumplings a few at a time into the boiling water on top of the chicken. If you put too many in the pot at once, they may stick together. Cook in the uncovered pot for 10 minutes; then cover them and cook 10 minutes longer. When done, put the dumplings and the chicken on the plate and serve. Makes 4 servings.

Sulphronia's
Southern Fried Chicken

from RABBIT HILL by Robert Lawson

"New Folks coming!" was the excited cry of all the animals on the Hill. For three years the gardens and lawns at the Big House had been neglected and food was getting scarce. But now the shiftless tenants were gone and new people were moving in. Little Georgie the Rabbit, Porkey the Woodchuck, Willie Fieldmouse—*all* the animals hoped they would be planters. And they were. There was food for everyone: bluegrass, carrots, peas, corn, grain, and kohlrabi. Even Phewie the skunk was satisfied—he'd never found such delicious things in the garbage before.

In the chicken-run countless baby chicks ran and scratched and peeped endlessly while the mother hens chuckled and scolded. Phewie and the Gray Fox often paused there in the early evenings to look over the prospects, but Phewie was so satisfied by Sulphronia [the cook's] generosity in the matter of garbage that his interest in live chicken was rapidly waning. He had even persuaded the Fox to sample a bit of her cookery. The Fox at first had scorned the idea, saying he preferred his chicken fresh, but after trying a Southern-fried chicken wing, as Sulphronia fried it, he had been quite won over, and now usually joined Phewie in his midnight feasts.

One of the great recipes of the South is . . . Southern fried chicken. Here is one old, tried and true recipe. We bet you won't have any left over to throw away.

INGREDIENTS	UTENSILS
Large can of	Frying pan
shortening	Large spoon
1 cup flour	Measuring cup
1 teaspoon salt	Measuring spoons
¼ teaspoon pepper	Medium-sized paper bag
1 large frying chicken,	Large fork
cut into pieces	Paper towels
	Plate

1. Put a frying pan on the stove and turn the heat on quite high. Melt enough shortening in the pan so that it is about 1 inch deep. When the shortening is melted, turn the heat down to medium.

2. Put the flour, salt, and pepper in a paper bag.

3. Rinse the chicken in cold water and shake off the excess water. Do not dry. Shake each piece separately in the bag, keeping the top closed very tight. When the pieces are well coated with flour, remove them and shake off most of the flour.

4. Very carefully place the chicken in the hot deep fat. Cook it for 15 to 20 minutes on each side until the pieces are golden brown, turning with a fork.

5. Place a paper towel on a plate, and as the chicken finishes frying, drain it quickly on the towel. Serve hot. Serves 4.

Tom's Fried Fish

from TOM SAWYER by Mark Twain

Tom was both the joy and the heartache of his Aunt Polly. He hated taking baths and going to school or church regularly, and he was always tempted by a new adventure! Once he and Huckleberry Finn and Joe Harper decided to run away from home and camp out like pirates. They spent the night steering a raft down the river to their chosen island and slept late the next morning, truly enjoying their freedom. A swim and then breakfast outdoors!

They came back to camp wonderfully refreshed, glad-hearted, and ravenous; and they soon had the campfire blazing up again. Huck found a spring of clear cold water close by, and the boys made cups of broad oak or hickory leaves and felt that water, sweetened with such a wildwood charm as that, would be a good enough substitute for coffee. While Joe was slicing bacon for breakfast, Tom and Huck asked him to hold on a minute; they stepped to a promising nook in the river bank and threw in their lines; almost immediately they had reward. Joe had not had time to get impatient before they were back again with some handsome bass, a couple of sun perch and a small catfish—provisions enough for quite a family. They fried the fish with the bacon and were astonished; for no fish had ever seemed so delicious before. They did not know that the quicker a fresh water fish is on the fire after he is caught the better he is; and they reflected little upon what a sauce open-air sleeping, open-air exercise, bathing, and a large ingredient of hunger makes, too.

It's a Southern custom to eat fried fish for breakfast, but most people have it for dinner. And it is true, the sooner you cook your fish after you've bought it, the sweeter it will taste.

INGREDIENTS	UTENSILS
½ cup flour	Measuring cup
4 fillets (pieces) of sole	Large plate
Salt	Large frying pan
Pepper	Measuring spoons
2 tablespoons butter	Metal spatula
1 lemon	Paring knife

1. Put the flour on a large plate. Carefully dust both sides of the pieces of fish with the flour and then sprinkle with salt and pepper.

2. Put a large frying pan on the stove and turn the heat to medium. Melt the butter in the pan until it sizzles, but do not let it turn brown.

3. Place the fish fillets in the pan and fry them on each side for about 5 minutes or until lightly browned. Turn them carefully with a spatula. When cooked, arrange on a platter. Cut the lemon in small wedges and serve. Makes 4 servings.

Jo's New England Boiled Dinner

from LITTLE WOMEN by Louisa May Alcott

Whether the four March sisters were putting on a play, writing a newsletter, or cooking a company dinner, the affair was sure to be delightful, and only occasionally disastrous. Meg, Beth, Jo, and Amy lived in the typical New England town of Concord, Massachusetts. Money was scarce, for their father had gone to war, and each of the girls had a job and helped out with chores around the house. One day when Hannah the cook was away, Jo impulsively decided to make dinner. To her sister's horror, she even invited Laurie, the handsome boy next door, as guest of honor.

*Y*ou'd better see what you have got before you think of having company," said Meg when informed of the hospitable but rash act.

45

"Oh, there's corned beef and plenty of potatoes, and I shall get some asparagus and a lobster, 'for a relish,' as Hannah says. We'll make a salad. I don't know how, but the books tell. I'll have blancmange and strawberries for dessert, and coffee too, if you want to be elegant."

"Don't try too many messes, Jo, for you can't make anything but gingerbread and molasses candy fit to eat. I wash my hands of the dinner party, and since you have asked Laurie on your own responsibility, you may just take care of him."

Jo's dinner turned out rather badly—she ended up with wilted asparagus, undercooked potatoes, and salty strawberries. The corned beef and potatoes she was planning to use are the main ingredients of a traditional New England boiled dinner, and if you follow the recipe carefully, you'll no doubt have more success than Jo.

INGREDIENTS	UTENSILS
3-lb. brisket of corned beef, tied	Large 3-quart kettle, with cover
½ bay leaf	Large spoon
6 peppercorns	Vegetable peeler
8 small white potatoes	Paring knife
4 medium turnips	Slotted spoon
4 medium carrots	Large fork
8 small onions	Platter
1 medium cabbage	

1. Put the beef in a large iron kettle and cover it with cold water. Add the bay leaf and peppercorns.

2. Place the kettle on the stove and turn the heat on high. Bring the water to the boiling point. If fat forms on top of the water, skim it off with a spoon. Cover the kettle, turn heat to medium, and simmer the meat for 2 hours.

3. When the meat has cooked for about an hour and 30 minutes begin preparing the vegetables. Peel the potatoes and wash them under cold water.

4. Peel the turnips and cut them into ½-inch slices.

5. Peel the carrots. Cut off the tops, but leave them whole.

6. Peel the skin off the onions. Leave them whole.

7. Slice the bottom off the cabbage and cut it into 6 wedges.

8. When the meat has cooked for 2 hours, add all the vegetables to the pot. Cover again and simmer for 30 minutes.

9. Place the meat on a large platter, using a large fork to lift it and with a slotted spoon, take the vegetables out of the kettle and arrange them around the meat. Remove the bay leaf and any peppercorns. Makes 8 servings.

The Queen of Hearts' Strawberry Tarts

from ALICE IN WONDERLAND
by Lewis Carroll

mpulsively followed the muttering White Rabbit down his
der the hedge and discovered a whole new, fantastic
onders. The inhabitants were all quite unbelievable.
ire Cat disappeared a little at a time, leaving only
Duchess' baby became a pig, and the members of
yal court turned out to be a pack of cards. And
the Knave of Hearts was accused of stealing
was certainly the strangest one Alice had

ccusation!" said the King.
bbit blew three blasts on the trumpet,
rchment scroll, and read as follows:

"*The Queen of Hearts, she made some tarts,*
All on a summer's day:
The Knave of Hearts, he stole those tarts,
And took them quite away!"

"*Consider your verdict,*" the King said to the jury.

"*Not yet, not yet!*" the Rabbit hastily interrupted. "*There's a great deal to come before that!*"

"*Call the first witness,*" said the King; and the White Rabbit blew three blasts on the trumpet, and called out, "*First Witness!*"

The first witness was the Hatter. He came in with a teacup in one hand and a piece of bread-and-butter in the other. "*I beg pardon, your majesty,*" he began, "*for bringing these in: but I hadn't quite finished my tea when I was sent for.*"

"*You ought to have finished,*" said the King. "*When did you begin?*"

The Hatter looked at the March Hare, who had followed him into the court, arm-in-arm with the Dormouse. "*Fourteenth of March, I think it was,*" he said.

"*Fifteenth,*" said the March Hare.

"*Sixteenth,*" added the Dormouse.

"*Write that down,*" the King said to the jury, and the jury eagerly wrote down all three dates on their slates, and then added them up, and reduced the answer to shillings and pence.

It may be difficult to learn who stole the Queen's tarts, but it is not difficult to make them by following the recipe. Keep them in a very safe place lest they be stolen, too!

INGREDIENTS

Pastry:
2 cups sifted flour
1 teaspoon salt
⅔ cup lard or shortening,
    room temperature
¼ cup water
Filling:
Jar of strawberry jam

UTENSILS

Flour sifter
Measuring cup
Measuring spoons
Medium-sized bowl
Dull knife
Breadboard
Rolling pin
Metal spatula
Fork
Baking sheet
Cooling rack

1. Light the oven and set at 450°.

2. Presift the flour. Sift the measured flour with the salt into a medium-sized mixing bowl. Add the soft lard or shortening.

3. Rub the flour and shortening lightly through your fingers until they are well-mixed—the crumbs should be the size of small peas.

4. Pour the water in very slowly, a little at a time, cutting it in with a dull knife until the pastry forms a ball.

5. Put a little flour on a breadboard so the pastry will not stick, and put the ball of pastry on the board. Roll it out in all directions with a floured rolling pin until you have a big 12-inch square. If the dough sticks to the rolling pin or breadboard, scrape it off carefully with the dull knife and sprinkle more flour on the pin and board.

6. With the dull knife, cut out 9 4-inch squares.

7. With the spatula, carefully loosen each of the squares from the breadboard. Put 1½ teaspoons of strawberry jam in the center of each square. Fold in half to make a triangle shape. Press the very outer edge all the way around with a fork to seal it shut.

8. Place the squares on an ungreased baking sheet, about an inch apart, for they puff up.

9. Place in the oven and bake for 10 minutes. Remove them with the spatula to a cooling rack. Cool slightly before eating, the jam is very hot. Makes 9 tarts.

The Secret Recipe for
Cold Lemon Soufflé

from THE SECRET GARDEN
by Frances Hodgson Burnett

When Mary first came to live at Misselthwaite Manor, her
cousin Colin was a sickly, spoiled boy who wasn't expected to
live. But within a few months, much to the surprise of the
housekeeper and Colin's doctor, the boy was rosy-cheeked and
healthy. You'll have to read the book to find out the *whole*
secret, but one of the reasons Colin looked so well was
the children's wonderful picnics in the secret garden—which
Dr. Craven and Mrs. Medlock knew nothing about.

*I*s *there any way in which those children can get food*
secretly?" Dr. Craven inquired of Mrs. Medlock.
  "There's no way unless they dig it out of the earth or

pick it off the trees," Mrs. Medlock answered. "They stay out in the grounds all day and see no one but each other. And if they want anything different to eat from what's sent up to them they need only ask for it."

"Well," said Dr. Craven, "so long as going without food agrees with them we need not disturb ourselves. The boy is a new creature."

"So is the girl," said Mrs. Medlock. "She's begun to be downright pretty since she's filled out and lost her ugly little sour look. Her hair's grown thick and healthy looking and she's got a bright color. The glummest, ill-natured little thing she used to be and now her and Master Colin laugh together like a pair of crazy young ones. Perhaps they're growing fat on that."

It wasn't laughing that was fattening the children. It was the wonderful food they were eating. Here is a recipe the children might have been making to fatten Colin up. The *secret* is that when you make a real soufflé, it rises very high as it bakes in the oven. This cold soufflé also rises very high, but without cooking it.

INGREDIENTS

Vegetable oil
1 envelope unflavored
   gelatin
¼ cup cold water
6 egg yolks
1 cup sugar
1½ tablespoons grated
   lemon rind
¾ cup fresh lemon juice
   (about 4 lemons) or
   bottled lemon juice
4 egg whites
1½ cups heavy cream,
   chilled

UTENSILS

Waxed paper
String
1½-pint (3-cup) soufflé
   dish—or any round dish
   with straight sides
2 measuring cups
3 medium-sized bowls
Beater
Measuring spoons
Grater
Juice squeezer
Medium-sized saucepan
Large spoon

54

1. Tear off a piece of waxed paper 24 inches long and fold it in half. Wipe it with oil and wrap it around the top of a 1½-pint soufflé dish so the paper stands about an inch above the dish, oiled side in. Fasten it in place with string.

2. In a measuring cup, mix the gelatin and water. Let stand until thick.

3. In a medium-sized bowl, separate the egg yolks from the whites and put 4 of the whites in another bowl. (Save the 2 extra egg whites for another recipe.)

4. Add the sugar to the egg yolks and beat with a beater until the mixture is thick and light.

5. Grate the lemon rind onto a piece of waxed paper and squeeze the lemon juice. Stir both into the egg-yolk mixture.

6. Pour the mixture into a saucepan and heat over low heat. Cook until thickened, stirring constantly with a large spoon.

7. Remove the saucepan from the stove and stir in the thickened gelatin mixture until the gelatin is dissolved.

8. Remove the pan from the heat and cool the mixture for at least 20 minutes. Stir occasionally.

9. Beat the egg whites with a beater until stiff. Fold them carefully into the cooled egg-yolk mixture.

10. In another bowl, whip the heavy cream with a beater until it is thick and stiff. Fold it carefully into the egg-yolk mixture.

11. Pour the mixture slowly into the 1½-pint dish. It should fill the dish almost to the top of the waxed paper.

12. Chill it in the refrigerator for at least 2 hours or until ready to serve. Remove the waxed paper carefully before serving. Makes 6 servings.

The Monkeys' Fruit Cocktail

from THE STORY OF DR. DOLITTLE
by Hugh Lofting

Dab-Dab the duck, Jip the dog, Gub-Gub the baby pig, Polynesia the parrot, and Too-Too the owl, all loved living with

Dr. Dolittle. But the Doctor's sister and patients complained so bitterly about his friends that he decided to give up treating people and become an animal doctor. Before long his fame spread throughout the animal kingdom, and he was asked to go as far away as Africa to treat the monkeys, who were dying by the hundreds of a strange illness. When all were well again, the Doctor told them that he must return home.

When the packing was finished and everything was ready to start, the monkeys gave a grand party for the Doctor, and all the animals of the jungle came. And they had pineapples and mangoes and honey and all sorts of good things to eat and drink.

After they had all finished eating, the Doctor got up and said, "My friends: I am not clever at speaking long words after dinner, like some men; and I have just eaten many fruits and much honey. But I wish to tell you that I am very sad at leaving your beautiful country. Because I have things to do in the Land of the White Men, I must go. After I have gone, remember never to let the flies settle on your food before you eat it; and do not sleep on the ground when the rains are coming. I—er—er—I hope you will all live happily ever after."

When the Doctor stopped speaking and sat down, all the monkeys clapped their hands a long time and said to one another, "Let it be remembered always among our people that he sat and ate with us, here, under the trees. For surely he is the Greatest of Men!"

What a wonderful tropical party they must have had! Instead of eating the fruits alone, they could have made a great fruit cocktail of pineapples, mangoes, and other fruits, laced with honey. But you can make it to serve before dinner or as a dessert. If you can't find all the fruits listed in the recipe, simply choose others that you like.

INGREDIENTS

1 medium-sized bunch
  seedless green grapes
2 ripe bananas
1 ripe fresh pineapple
  (or 1 medium-sized can
  pineapple chunks)
1 medium-sized can
  grapefruit sections
1 medium-sized can
  mandarin orange sections
8 maraschino cherries
1 mango (optional)
½ cup honey

UTENSILS

Large serving bowl
Sieve
Small paring knife
Large sharp knife
Can opener
Measuring cup
Large spoon

1. Take the grapes off their stems, put them in a sieve, and wash them. Put them in a serving bowl.

2. Peel the bananas, and cut them into thin slices, and put them in the bowl with the grapes.

3. If you have a fresh pineapple, use a large knife and first cut off the top and the bottom of the fruit. Then carefully cut away all the rough outside. Next cut away little pieces around the hard core and put them in the bowl. If you're using canned pineapple cubes, just open the can, drain off the juice, and put the cubes in the bowl.

4. Open the can of grapefruit, drain off the juice, and put the sections in the serving bowl. Do the same thing with the canned mandarin orange sections. Add the cherries.

5. If you have a fresh mango, use a small paring knife to cut away the skin. Then cut it into small thin slices and put them in the bowl. There is a large seed in the middle, so you cannot cut through the fruit.

6. Pour the honey over the fruit. With a large spoon, *very carefully* mix the fruit and honey. Put in the refrigerator to chill before serving. Makes 8 large servings.

Halloween Mocha Cake

from ONION JOHN by Joseph Krumgold

Onion John may have had strange ways—he lived in a house made of piled up stone with four bathtubs, he ate onions the way most people eat apples, and spoke a language that only Andy Rusch could understand. But his ways made sense to Andy, and Onion John was his best friend. It was Andy's idea to ask him to join the Halloween party that he and his three friends gave each year. But it was Onion John and his special ideas about spirits that changed the annual event that Halloween. Andy, Eech Ries, Bo Hemmendinger, and Bits Schwarz each chipped in for the decorations for the party, but the menu was always the same.

The main course is Mocha Cake which we have made to order down at Struhlmeyer's. It has to be a pretty big cake to hold all the writing on it, Good Wishes, Rusch, Schwarz, Hemmendinger, Ries. *Then there's éclairs which are chocolate and vanilla cream puffs. For other courses we have Napoleons and two kinds of ice cream and rice pudding. The rice pudding's mostly for Bo, so we have that first the way you'd start off with soup. On the side, we have two little paper cups at each place, one filled with salted nuts and the other with chocolate creams. To drink we have Kiowa Club Ginger Ale which stings your throat if it goes down fast and makes your nose itch. It gives you the feeling it could be hard liquor you were drinking and that's an excuse for acting drunk if you feel like it.*

The boys ate mocha cake for Halloween, but you can serve it any time. If you want to write your name or someone else's on the top, you can do that too.

INGREDIENTS

1 cup sugar
½ cup butter, room
   temperature
2 eggs
1 teaspoon vanilla
2 cups sifted flour
3 teaspoons baking
   powder
¼ teaspoon salt
¾ cup milk

UTENSILS

Measuring cup
Large bowl
Beater
Measuring spoons
Large spoon
Flour sifter
Plate
2 8-inch layer cake pans
Cooling rack

1. Light the oven and set at 375°.

2. Put the softened butter in a large bowl and gradually beat in the sugar with a beater until the mixture is light and creamy.

3. Crack the eggs on the side of the bowl, drop them in, and with the beater, beat them into the butter and sugar. Stir in the vanilla.

4. Presift the flour. Sift the measured flour with the baking powder and salt onto a plate.

5. Add the flour mixture and the milk alternately, a little at a time, to the butter mixture. Stir thoroughly after you add each small amount.

6. Grease 2 8-inch layer pans well. Pour half of the batter into each pan and spread evenly.

7. Bake the cake in the oven for 25 minutes. If the cake has baked long enough, the top of it will spring back when you touch it lightly with your finger.

8. Take the cake from the oven. Place a cooling rack on top and turn both rack and cake upside down. Cool on the rack for about 10 minutes before removing the cake pan. Then cool the cake on the rack before frosting.

MOCHA CREAM FROSTING

INGREDIENTS	UTENSILS
⅓ cup strong coffee	Coffee pot
⅓ cup butter (about ¾ of a stick)	Large size bowl
	Measuring cup
1 square unsweetened chocolate	Small saucepan
	Large spoon
4 cups confectioners' sugar (about 1 box)	Flour sifter
	Egg beater
1 teaspoon vanilla extract	Measuring spoons
Salt	Dull knife

1. Make coffee the way you do at home, but make it very strong.

2. Put the butter in a large size bowl and let it soften.

3. Place the square of chocolate in a small saucepan and over very low heat melt it very slowly. Stir it frequently as it can burn quickly. Set it aside.

4. Sift enough confectioners' sugar to measure 4 cups.

5. Beat the butter with an egg beater until very light and creamy.

6. Slowly beat in 2 cups of the sugar, mixing it well each time you add a little.

7. Add 1 teaspoon of vanilla extract and a pinch of salt.

8. Add in the melted chocolate, mixing well.

9. Slowly beat in the other 2 cups of sugar, adding the coffee with it to keep it moist.

10. Use a knife to frost the cake. First put some frosting on the top of one layer. Set the other layer on top of the first by holding it securely on each side. Frost the sides of the cake. Then spread the rest of the frosting on the top, swirling it to the edge. To set the frosting, chill for 30 minutes.

Captain Hook's Poison Cake

from PETER PAN by J. M. Barrie

Wendy, John, and Michael had a Newfoundland dog named Nana for a nurse. She was a wonderful guardian, and all went well until the night she was tied in the backyard. Peter Pan, the boy who wanted never to grow up, and Tinker Bell, his fairy friend, lured the children away to Neverland, the land of lost boys. They met a crocodile with a clock in its stomach, mermaids, and a band of redskins, but the most fearsome person there was Captain Hook. Peter had long ago cut off Hook's arm and fed it to the crocodile, so Hook wanted very much to get revenge. Here's one of his plots:

To return to the ship," Hook replied slowly through his teeth, "and cook a large rich cake of a jolly thickness with green sugar on it. . . . We will leave the cake on the shore of the mermaids' lagoon. These boys are always swimming about there, playing with the mermaids. They will find the cake and they will gobble it up, because, having no mother, they don't know how dangerous 'tis to eat rich damp cake." He burst into laughter, not hollow laughter now, but honest laughter. "Aha, they will die."

This is an utterly deadly wonderful cake!

INGREDIENTS

3 eggs
1 cup sugar
½ cup butter, room
  temperature
1½ cups sifted cake flour
¼ teaspoon salt
2 teaspoons baking powder
½ cup milk
½ teaspoon vanilla

UTENSILS

Large bowl
Beater
Measuring cup
Large spoon
Medium-sized bowl
Flour sifter
Plate
Measuring spoons
9-inch cake pan
Cooling rack

1. Light the oven and set at 350°.

2. Separate the egg yolks from the whites and put the whites in a large bowl. Beat the whites with a beater until stiff. When the whites are stiff enough, peaks will form on the top that stand alone when the beater is raised. (Save the yolks for another recipe.)

3. With a large spoon, fold ½ cup of the sugar into the whites, a little at a time.

4. Put the softened butter in a medium-sized bowl. Gradually beat in the other ½ cup of sugar until the mixture is light and creamy.

5. Presift the flour. Sift the measured flour with the salt and baking powder onto a plate.

6. Add the flour mixture and the milk alternately, a little at a time, to the creamed butter and sugar. Stir after you add each small amount.

7. Fold in the egg whites very gently.

8. Stir in the vanilla.

9. Pour the batter into a greased cake pan and bake in the oven 1 hour. If the cake has baked long enough, the top of it will spring back when you touch it lightly with your finger.

10. Take the cake from the oven. Place a cooling rack on top of the cake and turn both rack and cake upside down. Cool on the rack for about 10 minutes before removing the cake pan. Then cool the cake on the rack before frosting. This makes a low but light cake.

GREEN FROSTING

INGREDIENTS
¼ cup light cream
1¾ cups confectioners' sugar
1 teaspoon vanilla
Green coloring

UTENSILS
Measuring cup
Medium-sized bowl
Large spoon
Flour sifter
Measuring spoons
Dull knife

1. Put the cream in a medium-sized bowl. Sift the sugar into the cream and beat with a spoon for about 3 minutes until the mixture is very light and thick enough to spread.

2. Stir in the vanilla and a few drops of green coloring.

3. Use a knife to frost the cake. First put some frosting on the sides of the cake. Then spread the rest on the top, swirling it to the edge.

Mrs. Cratchit's Christmas Date Pudding

from A CHRISTMAS CAROL
by Charles Dickens

"Bah! Humbug!" said Ebenezer Scrooge. "Every idiot who goes about with 'Merry Christmas' on his lips should be boiled with his own pudding." But that night Scrooge was visited by the ghost of his long dead partner, Marley, and warned to change his stingy ways or be doomed forever. He was shown Christmas Past and a scene from his early manhood when his employer always gave a joyous celebration on Christmas Eve. Then he was shown a vision of Christmas Present and the family of his miserably underpaid clerk, Bob Cratchit, with their small crippled son, Tiny Tim, keeping the true and generous spirit of Christmas even though they were poor. Mrs. Cratchit cooked a wonderful holiday dinner—here is a description of just the dessert!

69

But now, the plates being changed by Miss Belinda, Mrs. Cratchit left the room alone—too nervous to bear witnesses— to take the pudding up and bring it in. Suppose it should not be done enough! Suppose it should break in turning it out! Suppose somebody should have got over the wall of the back-yard, and stolen it, while they were merry with the goose—a supposition at which the two young Cratchits became livid! All sorts of horrors were supposed. Hallo! A great deal of steam! The pudding was out of the copper. A smell like a washing-day! That was the cloth. A smell like an eating-house and a pastry-cook's next door to each other, with a laundress's next door to that! That was the pudding! In half a minute Mrs. Cratchit entered—flushed, but smiling proudly—with the pudding, like a speckled cannonball, so hard and firm, blazing in half of half-a-quatern of ignited brandy, and bedight with Christmas holly stuck into the top. Oh, a wonderful pudding! Bob Cratchit said, and calmly too, that he regarded it as the greatest success achieved by Mrs. Cratchit since their marriage. Mrs. Cratchit said that now the weight was off her mind, she would confess she had had her doubts about the quantity of flour. Everybody had something to say about it, but nobody said or thought it was at all a small pudding for a large family. It would have been heresy to do so. Any Cratchit would have blushed to hint at such a thing.

You, too, can make this wonderful pudding for the holiday. You can bring it in blazing as Mrs. Cratchit did or serve it with a lemon sauce. You can make one large pudding, but it's easier to make in individual cups.

INGREDIENTS	UTENSILS
3 tablespoons butter	Measuring spoons
½ cup molasses	Small saucepan
1 cup milk	Measuring cup
1 ⅞ cups flour	Large spoon
½ teaspoon baking soda	Flour sifter
¼ teaspoon salt	Medium-sized bowl
¼ teaspoon ground clove	Paring knife
¼ teaspoon nutmeg	8 custard cups
½ pound pitted dates	Aluminum foil
¼ cup chopped nuts	Shallow pan

1. Light the oven and set at 350°.

2. Melt the butter in a small saucepan and add the molasses and milk. Stir thoroughly over low heat.

3. Presift the flour. Sift the measured flour, baking soda, salt, ground clove, and nutmeg together into a medium-sized bowl.

4. Add the molasses mixture to the dry ingredients.

5. Cut the dates into fine pieces and add the dates and the chopped nuts to the mixture.

6. Butter 8 custard cups and fill them ⅔ full with the mixture. Cover each with a piece of aluminum foil.

7. Fill a shallow pan with 1 inch of water. Set the custard cups in the pan and put it in the oven. Cook for 2½ hours. Check occasionally to be sure the water has not evaporated.

8. When cooked, remove the pan from the oven with 2 pot holders. Remove the custard cups and carefully empty the hot water from the pan. Fill the pan with the same amount of cold

water—about 1 inch—and set the cups in the water for a few minutes to cool quickly. Then turn each custard cup upside down on an individual plate and remove the cup. Top with Thin Lemon Sauce. Makes 8 servings.

THIN LEMON SAUCE

INGREDIENTS

¾ cup sugar
2 tablespoons light corn
  syrup
¼ cup water
2 teaspoons butter
1 tablespoon lemon juice

UTENSILS

Medium-sized saucepan
Measuring cup
Measuring spoons
Large spoon

1. In a saucepan, bring the sugar, corn syrup, and water to a boil. Boil for 5 minutes without stirring.

2. Remove from stove. Mix in the butter and lemon juice and pour some sauce on top of each pudding.

Ma's Pumpkin Pie

from LITTLE HOUSE IN THE BIG WOODS
by Laura Ingalls Wilder

In the Big Woods of Wisconsin stood the little log house where Laura and Mary lived with their Pa and Ma and baby sister Carrie. It was 1872 and town was a good day's trip away, so the family had to provide for themselves. They planted their own garden with potatoes, carrots, and onions; made their own butter and cheese; and smoked their own deer and bear meat. Fall was a particularly busy time for everyone. With winter coming, all the food they would need until the next spring had to be stored away.

Laura and Mary helped, picking up the dusty potatoes after Pa had dug them from the ground, and pulling the long yellow carrots and the round, purple-topped turnips, and they helped Ma cook the pumpkin for pumpkin pies.
With the butcher knife Ma cut the big, orange-colored

73

pumpkins into halves. She cleaned the seeds out of the center and cut the pumpkin into long slices, from which she pared the rind. Laura helped her cut the slices into cubes.

Ma put the cubes into the big iron pot on the stove, poured in some water, and then watched while the pumpkin slowly boiled down, all day long. All the water and the juice must be boiled away, and the pumpkin must never burn.

The pumpkin was a thick, dark, good-smelling mass in the kettle. It did not boil like water, but bubbles came up in it and suddenly exploded, leaving holes that closed quickly. Every time a bubble exploded, the rich, hot, pumpkin smell came out.

Laura stood on a chair and watched the pumpkin for Ma, and stirred it with a wooden paddle. She held the paddle in both hands and stirred carefully, because if the pumpkin burned there wouldn't be any pumpkin pies.

Pumpkin pies are tasty in the fall. You can fix your own pumpkin as they did in Wisconsin or you can start with some canned pumpkin, which is easier, and still make a wonderful pie. This is my grandmother's old-fashioned recipe:

INGREDIENTS

Pie shell:
2 cups sifted flour
1 teaspoon salt
⅔ cup lard or shortening, room temperature
¼ cup water

Filling:
2 eggs
2 cups canned pumpkin
1 cup sugar
1 tablespoon flour
1 teaspoon salt
1 teaspoon cinnamon
1 teaspoon nutmeg
1 teaspoon ginger
3 tablespoons molasses
2 cups milk

UTENSILS

Flour sifter
2 measuring cups
Measuring spoons
Medium-sized bowl
Dull knife
Breadboard
Rolling pin
9-inch piepan
Large bowl
Fork
Large spoon
Can opener

74

1. Light the oven and set at 425°.

2. Presift the flour. Sift the measured flour with the salt into a medium-sized bowl. Add the soft lard or shortening.

3. Rub the flour and shortening lightly through your fingers until they are well-mixed—the crumbs should be the size of small peas.

4. Pour the water in very slowly, a little at a time, cutting it in with a dull knife until the pastry forms a ball.

5. Sprinkle some flour on a breadboard so the pastry will not stick and put the ball of pastry on the board. Flatten it a little with your hand. Roll it out lightly with a floured rolling pin until you have an 11-inch circle. If the dough sticks to the rolling pin or breadboard, scrape it off carefully with a dull knife and sprinkle more flour on the pin and board.

6. Fold the circle of pastry in half. Lift it halfway into the piepan and then unfold the other half over the rest of the pan. Carefully arrange the dough so it lines the pan. With a fork, press down the pastry edge all the way around the pan. Cut off any piecrust that hangs over the edge.

7. To make the filling, crack the eggs on the edge of a large mixing bowl and drop them in. Beat them lightly with a fork. Add the pumpkin and mix it with the eggs. Add the sugar, flour, salt, cinnamon, nutmeg, ginger, molasses, and milk and mix well.

8. Pour the mixture into the piecrust. (You may have a little left over.) Put the pie in the oven and bake for 15 minutes or until the crust is brown. Then turn the heat down to 375° and bake for about one hour, or until the filling is firm. Test by shaking the pan lightly—if the filling doesn't jiggle, the pie is done. Serve hot or cold. Makes 6 or 7 servings.

Mrs. Gilligan's Griddle Bread

from ROLLER SKATES by Ruth Sawyer

Patrick Gilligan took Lucinda in his hansom cab to the home of Misses Peters and Nettie, where she was going to live for a year while her parents were in Europe. It was to be a glorious year, with the freedom to explore New York City on her roller skates, and Mr. Gilligan was only the first of many wonderful new friends. As she chatted with him, she guessed that he was Irish and asked if he had ever eaten griddle bread with currants in it. . . . Indeed he had, for it was one of his favorite dishes. Secretly, Lucinda wished he and his wife would ask her to share it with them some evening. And later that year, they did.

They found Mrs. Gilligan greasing the griddle and washing the currants. Lucinda went into the kitchen to help and ex-

plained to Mrs. Gilligan that she was glad they didn't have a dining-room; she never yet had eaten griddle bread outside a kitchen, and she never could. Mrs. Gilligan was round as a dumpling, red as an apple; her hair was combed upwards and ended in a doughnut on the top of her head. She called Lucinda "wee lamb," and Lucinda got jumbled in her thinking trying to decide whether Mrs. Gilligan looked like Johanna [Lucinda's Irish nurse] grown old, or Johanna looked like Mrs. Gilligan grown young. The kitchen was snug and the right size for three. There were candles on the table, and a red geranium, grown from slips. There were ham and Irish potatoes, gooseberry jam, and the griddle bread. Lucinda hung over the stove as it cooked and watched the currants come to the top and pop through: Cut pie-ways, she and Mr. Gilligan ran a race with the butter to see who could spread on the most. After it was eaten down to the last slice, and not a crumb left for Miss Manners, Lucinda took the guitar out of its case and sang those Irish songs she had had from Johanna.

Doesn't it sound like a wonderful Irish dish? Lots of butter and lots of currants and a good appetite are all you need!

INGREDIENTS	UTENSILS
4 tablespoons butter	Measuring spoons
4 cups flour	Measuring cup
1 teaspoon salt	Large bowl
1 teaspoon baking soda	Large spoon
½ cup currants or raisins	Breadboard
1¼ cups milk	Dull knife
	Frying pan
	Metal spatula

1. Put the flour and 1 tablespoon of butter in a large bowl. Rub them together lightly through your fingers until they are well-mixed.

2. Add the salt and baking soda and mix well.

3. Add the currants or raisins.

78

4. Add the milk and stir it into the mixture until the dough forms a ball.

5. Put the ball of dough on a floured breadboard. Flatten it out with your hands into a large circle 1-inch thick. Cut the circle into quarters.

6. Put a frying pan on the stove and turn the heat on low. Melt the remaining butter in the frying pan. Put the quarters or farls, as they are known in Ireland, in the frying pan and cook over a low heat for 15 to 20 minutes on each side until they are lightly browned. Turn them with a spatula. Serve with lots of butter. Makes 4 servings.

Robinson Crusoe's
Homemade Oven Bread

from ROBINSON CRUSOE by Daniel Defoe

Robinson Crusoe didn't listen to the advice of his father to
settle down to a comfortable life in the English town where he
grew up. Instead he ran away to sea. On one of his voyages
the ship was ripped apart in a storm, and he found himself
the only survivor on a tropical island. He built a crude home
for himself and then set about learning how to provide for his
bare needs by hunting and farming. When he'd successfully
raised a crop of grain, and discovered how to make fireproof
pots, he felt ready to try baking some bread.

*When the firewood was burnt pretty much into embers, or
live coals, I drew them forward upon the hearth, so as to
cover it all over, and there I let them lie, till the hearth was
very hot; then sweeping away all the embers, I set down my*

loaf, or loaves; and whelming down the earthen pot upon them, drew the embers all round outside of the pot, to keep in, and add to the heat. And thus, as well as in the best oven in the world, I baked my barley loaves, .and became in a little time a pastry cook into the bargain, for I made myself several cakes of the rice, and puddings.

Robinson Crusoe had to go to a great deal of trouble to make his bread. With a little time you can make some homemade oven-baked bread, too—with much less effort!

INGREDIENTS
2 cups milk
1 cake or package of yeast
2 tablespoons sugar
1 tablespoon salt
6 cups sifted flour
3 tablespoons butter

UTENSILS
Measuring cup
Saucepan
Large bowl
Measuring spoons
Large spoon, preferably
    wooden
Flour sifter
Small saucepan
Dish towel
Breadboard
2 5×10-inch loaf pans
Cooling racks

1. Warm the milk in a saucepan and pour into a large bowl. Sprinkle in the yeast, sugar, and salt. Stir until dissolved.

2. Presift the flour. Sift the measured flour gradually and mix into the liquid.

3. Melt the butter in a saucepan over low heat and stir it into the dough until the dough is shiny. Cover with a dish towel and let the dough rest 10 minutes.

4. Put a little flour on a breadboard. Put the dough on the board and press it flat. Knead by folding the farthest edge of the dough toward you (fold the dough in half) and working

the fold into the dough with the heels of your hands. Turn the dough around a little on the board and repeat. Knead for 10 to 15 minutes until the dough has a silky look.

5. Put the kneaded dough back in the large bowl and cover the bowl with a clean dish towel. Place it in a warm dark place and let it rise for an hour and a half.

6. Again, put a light covering of flour on the breadboard, take out the dough, and knead as before for about 15 minutes. Shape into two little loaves, to fit 5×10-inch pans.

7. Grease the bread pans with butter and put the dough in the pans. Cover again with the dish towel, put it back in a warm, dark spot, and let the dough rise for about an hour, or until it has doubled in size.

8. Light the oven and set for 375°. When the bread has risen for the hour, put it in the oven and bake for 40 minutes. When baked, remove from oven, put a cooling rack on top of each pan, and turn upside down. Remove pan. Cool the bread on the rack before serving.

Pennsylvania Pretzels

from THEE, HANNAH! by Marguerite de Angeli

Hannah lived in Philadelphia, and her family were Quakers, who believed that the beauty in life came from one's inner feelings and not from owning beautiful things. But Hannah loved pretty clothes, and she wished that her plain dress and heavy Quaker bonnet were made with satin and lace and flowers. You'll have to read the book to find out how important the hated bonnet became to Hannah, why one day it suddenly felt light and beautiful. In the meantime, you can make the wonderful pretzels she used to buy from the vendor on the streets and on the frozen river where she skated.

When they reached the river, Sally, Hannah and Cecily sat on the edge of the wharf while the boys helped them on with their skates.

Boats that had been caught in the sudden cold were frozen at the wharf. Besides the skaters, horses and sleighs went up and down the frozen river, and vendors of every kind cried their wares. A woman sold pepper-pot from a wagon; the pretzel man pushed his cart over the ice; the muffin woman carried her basket on her head. A crowd of young people had even built a fire on the ice. There hadn't been a freeze like it for years!

Pennsylvania pretzels can be eaten fresh and warm with mustard. Did you know that the curls of the pretzels represent angels with their arms crossed over their heads in a prayer of supplication?

INGREDIENTS

1 cup warm water
3 packages of yeast
3 cups flour
2 teaspoons baking soda
1 egg
Coarse salt
Caraway seeds

UTENSILS

Measuring cup
Large mixing bowl
Large spoon
Breadboard
Dish towel
Large shallow pan
Measuring spoons
Rolling pin
Dull knife
Slotted spatula
Cookie sheet
Small bowl
Fork
Pastry brush

1. Light the oven and set it at 400°.

2. Put the cup of warm water and all the yeast into a large mixing bowl. Stir until the yeast is dissolved.

3. Gradually add the flour to the yeast mixture. When all the flour has been added, you will have a very stiff dough.

4. Sprinkle a little flour on a breadboard and put the dough on the board. Knead by folding the farthest edge of the dough

toward you (fold the dough in half) and working the fold into the dough with the heels of your hands. Turn the dough around a little and repeat. Knead for 5 minutes.

5. Make the dough into a ball and put it back into the bowl. Cover the bowl with a clean dish towel and let it stand in a warm, dark place for about 30 minutes.

6. While you are waiting for the dough to rise, fill a large shallow pan half full of water, add the baking soda, and bring it to a simmer.

7. After the dough has risen, put it on the breadboard again. Punch it gently until the air is let out. Then roll it with a rolling pin into a 6-inch square. With a dull knife, cut the dough into strips about the size of your finger. Twist each strip into a pretzel shape and pinch the ends together.

8. Slip the pretzels one at a time into the simmering water. They will sink to the bottom of the pan and then rise to the surface. Take them out of the pan with a slotted spatula and place them a few inches apart onto a greased cookie sheet. You will have to work carefully because the pretzels are very slippery at this stage.

9. Beat an egg with a fork in a small bowl. Using your pastry brush, brush each pretzel with the egg. Then sprinkle the coarse salt or caraway seeds over the pretzels. Bake them until they are golden brown, about 15 minutes. They will be soft rather than brittle.

Rat's Baked Ham

from THE WIND IN THE WILLOWS
by Kenneth Grahame

Mole worked hard all morning cleaning, but it was spring
and suddenly he flung his brush on the floor, "said 'Bother!'
and 'O Blow' and also 'Hang spring cleaning!' and bolted
out of the house." Strolling happily through the meadow in
the warm sunshine, he suddenly came upon a river. He'd never
seen one before, and he sat down to watch, fascinated by this
swirling, gurgling, chattering thing. All at once he found himself staring at the small, brown, whiskered face of Water Rat,
who promptly invited Mole to take a row in his boat with
him down the river. Mole couldn't have been more delighted.

*H*old hard a minute, then!" said the Rat. He looped the
painter through a ring in his landing-stage, climbed up into his
hole above, and after a short interval reappeared staggering
under a fat, wicker luncheon-basket.

"Shove that under your feet," he observed to the Mole, as he passed it down into the boat. Then he untied the painter and took the sculls again.

"What's inside it?" asked the Mole, wiggling with curiosity.

"There's cold chicken inside it," replied the Rat briefly; *"coldtonguecoldhamcoldbeefpickledgherkinssaladfrenchrollscress andwidgespottedmeatgingerbeerlemonadesodawater—"*

"O stop, stop," cried the Mole in ecstasies: *"This is too much!"*

What fun to plan a picnic with Rat's wonderful surprises! Cold sliced ham, which you can eat in sandwiches or by itself, would make an excellent start. Then you can put anything else you like in your picnic basket—such as picklesandlemonade andfrenchrollsand. . . .

INGREDIENTS

1 (1-lb.) precooked canned ham
12 whole cloves
1 tablespoon or 3 teaspoons prepared mustard
¼ cup brown sugar

UTENSILS

Can opener
Plate
Dull knife
Small roasting pan with rack
Paring knife
Small bowl
Measuring cup
Measuring spoons
Large spoon
Carving knife

1. Light the oven and set the temperature at 375° or according to the directions on the canned ham.

2. Open the can carefully and remove the ham onto a plate. Using a dull knife scrape off any jelly that might be around the ham. Place the meat on a rack in a roasting pan.

3. With a paring knife, make small crisscross cuts on the top of the meat. Put a whole clove in twelve of the crosses.

4. In a small bowl, mix the mustard and the brown sugar. Cover the top and sides of the ham with the mixture.

5. Put the ham in the oven and cook according to the directions given, or until heated through thoroughly, about 30 minutes. When it is done, cool and slice it carefully. Makes approximately 8 slices.

Glossary

BAKE: To cook in the oven away from direct flame.

BEAT: To work a mixture quickly with a spoon, hand beater, or electric mixer to make it smooth and light.

BOIL: To cook food in a liquid at boiling temperature— when bubbles constantly rise to the surface and break.

CREAM: To beat shortening with a spoon or an electric mixer until it is light and fluffy. You often work sugar into shortening to get a creamy mixture.

DISSOLVE: To mix a dry ingredient, such as yeast, into a liquid, such as water, until they are completely combined.

FOLD: To mix in ingredients such as egg whites or whipped cream with a gentle over-and-under motion. The technique is to use a spoon or rubber spatula and cut down through the batter to the bottom of the bowl. Turn the spatula and bring it up against the side of the bowl, folding some of the batter over the egg whites (or whatever ingredient you are folding in). Repeat until the egg whites are thoroughly mixed into the batter.

FRY: To cook in hot fat. To deep fry is to cook food in a large, deep pan with enough hot fat or salad oil to float the food.

GRATE: To rub food such as lemon rind or cheese on a grater to make little particles.

GREASE: To cover carefully the bottom and sides of a pan with shortening or butter to prevent the food from sticking to the pan.

KNEAD: To work dough with your hands. The technique is to fold the farthest edge of the dough toward you (fold the dough in half) and work the fold into the rest of the dough with the heels of your hands. Turn the dough around a little on the breadboard and repeat as directed in the recipe. If the dough becomes sticky, sprinkle a little flour on the board and on your hands.

PARE: To cut off the outer skin of a fruit or vegetable, usually with a knife.

PEEL: To pull off the outer skin of a fruit, such as bananas.

POACH: To simmer in a small amount of water.

ROLL: To spread out dough or pastry with a rolling pin. The technique is to sprinkle some flour on a breadboard to prevent the dough from sticking and place the dough on the board. Pat it into a ball and then flatten it with your hand. Flour the rolling pin slightly, and then begin to roll by pushing the dough out in all directions to form a large circle of the right thickness and size.

SEPARATE (EGGS): To divide the egg yolk from the egg white. The easiest method is to crack the egg across its middle on the side of a bowl or pan. Catch the yolk in one half of the shell, allowing the whites to drop into the bowl. Then carefully slip the yolk into the other half of the shell, letting the remaining whites drip into the bowl. The sharp edge of the shell helps to cut the whites away from the yolk. Be careful not to let *any* yolk get into the whites, as the whites will not beat up well if you do.

SIFT: To put dry ingredients, such as flour, sugar, and salt, through a flour sifter or fine sieve. In making cakes and piecrust, the flour is sifted twice. You sift the first time (*presift*) to introduce air in, making the flour light. In presifting, always put more than the desired amount of flour into the sifter. If you sift into a piepan, the flour won't spill over the work area and you can leave the sifter in the pan without washing it each time you use it. In the second sifting, the measured flour is combined with the other dry ingredients.

SIMMER: To cook in a liquid that is just below the boiling point—tiny bubbles will appear on the top of the liquid.

STIR: To mix ingredients round and round with a spoon.

WHIP: To beat rapidly with a rotary hand beater or electric mixer to trap air in the ingredients. To whip cream, beat very rapidly until it thickens and stiffens. To test, raise the beaters—if the cream mounds and holds it shape, it's whipped. If you're whipping cream in warm weather, be sure to chill the bowl and cream.

ABOUT THE AUTHOR

Carol MacGregor's love for cooking dates back to her own childhood when she helped her grandmother prepare the puddings and pies that made their country restaurant in New England famous. A gourmet cook, she makes a hobby of exploring and testing new recipes. Miss MacGregor attended Wheaton College and Columbia University, where she received a master's degree. She lives in New York City.

ABOUT THE ARTIST

Ray Cruz grew up in New York City and attended Pratt Institute and Cooper Union, where he received a degree in Fine and Graphic Arts. In addition to his work in book illustration, Mr. Cruz has done murals and is well known as a textile designer.

DATE DUE

641.5   **MacGregor, Carol**
M   The storybook cookbook

DATE DUE	BORROWER'S NAME	
11/17/69	Lu ann Shoop	
12/2/69	Lu ann Shoop	Jan 5
Jan 13		

641.5   **MacGregor, Carol**
M   The storybook cookbook

B 18-718